About the Author

Larry Borowitz lives in Johannesburg, South Africa. He has university degree in Information Systems and is a certified Lean Six Sigma Master Black Belt. Working in some of South Africa's leading companies, he has applied his broad skill set, experience and knowledge in different leadership, best practice, systems and consulting capacities. Larry has used his varied interests and creative talents to write one hundred poems in two years, the second set of which is published in this book, *Poetry in the Pandemic, Volume II*. Larry is married with three children.

Poetry in the Pandemic
Volume II

Larry Borowitz

Poetry in the Pandemic: Volume II

Olympia Publishers
London

www.olympiapublishers.com
OLYMPIA PAPERBACK EDITION

A CIP catalogue record for this title is
available from the British Library.

ISBN: 978 1-80439-248-5

This is a work of fiction.
Names, characters, places and incidents originate from the writer's
imagination. Any resemblance to actual persons, living or dead, is
purely coincidental.

First Published in 2023

Olympia Publishers
Tallis House
2 Tallis Street
London
EC4Y 0AB

Printed in Great Britain

Dedication

To:
My mother — whose values continue to guide;
My late father — who so loved the written word;
My brothers — for their friendship and laughter;
The fallen — in the battles of war.

Contents

Introduction 11

Change 13

Freedom 14

The Long Haul 15

Oxygen 16

Truth 17

Ruin 18

Differences 19

Senses 20

Fatigue 21

Darkness 22

Variants 23

Regrets 24

Minds, Bodies and Souls 25

Luck 26

Weeping 28

If Only… 30

Winning 32

Hesitancy 33

Liberty 35

Youth 36

Convince 38

Twenty Years on… 39

Mandate 41

Supply Chain 43

Choices 44

Booster 45

Borders 47

Reckoning 48

Cures 49
Junior Jab 50
Whiplash 51
Focal Point 52
Be Gentle 53
Wildfire 55
Relief 56
Time 57
Rights 58
Control 60
Rules 62
Work 63
Companions 64
Take-out / Take-in 65
Protests 66
Power 68
The Chess Game 70
Hero 72
Casualties 74
The Drumbeat 76
Two Years on… 77
The Human Spirit 79

Introduction

The Invisible War. The phrase I use to describe the COVID-19 pandemic. A war where humanity cannot see its enemy but uses all its ingenuity and tactics in combat.

As I write, the Invisible War is still being waged but its impact on the daily lives on the majority of the world's citizens has diminished and the death rate associated to COVID-19 has dropped dramatically. A number of factors — like vaccines and the inherent nature of a virus to mutate — enabled many battles to be successfully fought, but there is still the War to be won.

Poetry in the Pandemic, Volume II is an anthology of fifty poems which describes what it has been like to live through the second year of the COVID-19 pandemic.

After publishing *Poetry in the Pandemic,* which related to the first year of the pandemic, I decided to continue writing a poem every week and post these on Facebook, hoping to publish a second anthology. I am grateful that this has now come to fruition.

The second year of the pandemic was in many ways more challenging than the first. While the vaccines were a modern-day wonder which helped saved countless lives, the new variants and unwillingness by many to be vaccinated caused unnecessary death and suffering. The rollout of vaccines presented multiple challenges across different countries with varying strategies and adoption rates — often with dire consequences.

The geo-political landscape was also tested in many

regions of the world — with long-held antipathies flaring up and causing additional loss of life. The invasion of Ukraine by Russia has been an additional blight on the world with the consequences of that war currently being felt far and wide.

On a personal level, I was vaccinated as soon as the opportunity arose and have been fortunate not to have been infected by COVID-19, staying healthy and sticking to an exercise routine.

While writing these poems, I wanted to capture my weekly thoughts and feelings of what was happening during this seminal period of the twenty-first century. As I now read them as a full anthology, I reflect on a time of tragedy and hope, obstinacy and open-mindedness, setbacks and resilience and humanity at its worst and best.

The long-term impact of COVID-19 continues to be felt — the millions of families who miss their loved ones every day, those suffering from "long COVID", shifts in global trade patterns and changes to the world of work, to name a few. Its influence is here to stay.

I hope, no matter where or when you read these poems, you gain a deeper insight into what transpired during this unique time and how the world transformed. Yet, while the pandemic changed much, there is still much to change.

Larry Borowitz
20 June 2022

Change

If we must, we can
If we want, we will
If we should, we might
If we could, we may

Change
A constant
Sometimes embraced
Hard to do

If it's wrong, make it right
If it's bad, make it good
If it's hurt, make it heal
If it's hate, make it love

Change
One year on
Faster than expected
Willing or not

If it's physical, virtualise it
If it's unmasked, cover it
If it's close, distance it
If it's prejudiced, confront it

Change
In its vortex
Its effects
Here to stay…

Freedom

As the full moon lit the earth's corners
Degrees of freedom within different borders

The Ever Given afloat thanks to tugs and tides
The Suez Canal now open again on all sides

The Israelis got together to celebrate Passover
Leading the world with containing exposure

Vaccines being rolled out at record pace
Changing the trajectory in the United States

In March, Brazil's death toll its highest on record
France back in lockdown — rising cases not ignored

Sixty percent of the UK have received their first shots
Other parts of Europe, lagging with their citizens' slots

In South Africa, the spread of the virus has slowed
Will the third wave come before the vaccine is bestowed?

A very different picture compared to this time last year
Progress made in pockets to make the virus disappear

While we take steps towards living as we wish once more
Freedom will be achieved once we have all won the War.

Truth

Saris bathed in bewildered weary tears
Anguish etched into facial lines
Bent frames carrying a nation's fears
Fearing dreaded "Out of stock" signs

New infections at an alarming rate
Desperation for those distressed
Many helpless to change their luckless fate
As air in their lungs dispossessed

Patiently waiting a final farewell
In rows of funeral pyres
The departed have left the living hell
Their remains alight in the fires

Families struck — the aged and the youth
Many with woe are overcome
Hindu verse says "Death is the only truth"
Of the living what will become?

Ruin

As the Invisible War was waning, another began
Salvos spewed across the night sky like fireflies
Most caught by an iron net;
Some evade detection, achieving their game plan
Killing and maiming those whom they despise
An ever-present threat

Retaliation to destroy the places of terror —
Where funds were diverted from butter to guns
Hidden from view in a "metro";
Technology used to reduce the chance of error
Warnings given so they can save their sons
New strategies provide a lethal blow

Out of this cycle of destruction, anger and hate
So much senseless loss and pain
Heads and hearts harden;
Neighbours turn on each other to mutilate
Old friendships come under strain
Behaviours will be hard to pardon

Is this pattern bound to be repeated?
Is this what every generation must endure?
Is the enmity too ingrained?
When the mantra of destruction is deleted
When rights are recognised and secure
Will this swamp of ruin be drained.

Differences

When citizens were equally vulnerable
And shared an enemy so unassailable
Our common humanity was undeniable
To the virus we were all recognisable

Hoping for a world more agreeable
Naively denying the inevitable?
Suspended conflicts so intractable
Flare up in conflagrations flammable

Deep-seated prejudice unconscionable
Surfaces like a foe so implacable
Is this resurgence all too predictable?
Dredging up old tropes so despicable

One-sided reporting clearly observable
Selective facts identify the "blameable"
Empathy not shared in amounts equitable
Assaults stoked in places once thought improbable

The globe is battling this bug so intractable
Cooperation will make it conquerable
Loathing and war distract from the resolvable
Respect will produce outcomes more favourable.

Senses

Touch — limited to yourself and those you trust
Forbidden to freely hug feels so unjust
Suspicious of every surface you handle
Sanitised hands avoid personal scandal

Taste — the bliss of a delicious tasty treat
Continuously checking every bite you eat
Anxious the sensation will soon disappear
A first sign the virus' infection is here

Smell — identifying your surroundings and place
A mask conceals your nose from view, on your face
Suddenly absent from daily use and life
Gone for some months causing confusion and strife

Hear — ears open to what is meant to be said
Listen more to messages inside your head
Ignoring the words meant to protect and save
Could be the new harbinger of the third wave

Sight — for many, much suffering has been seen
Waiting patiently to receive the vaccine
Each has observed their worlds change before their eyes…
Waiting for each sensation to normalise.

Fatigue

Wearily trudging through
As months repeated;
Masks and distance protect
From the enemy unseen

With human destruction
Peaking in merciless waves;
We waited to be rescued
By the miraculous vaccine

The captivity ended
For some held hostage;
Yet in their state of slumber
Many can only dream

Waking up restless
From nightmares unending;
Tired of others' instructions
Locked down or in quarantine

Acts of defiance
A craving for the old normal;
Dropping one's guard
More affected if under eighteen

As liberation takes too long
Authorities relax the rules;
As fatigue leads to regret
Of what could have been.

Darkness

Dastardly darkness descends
South shores suffocating
Planned power pauses
Melancholy moods manifest

Farewell fellow friends
Relatives released reluctantly
Tired tidal tears
Unwanted upset ushered

Winter without warmth
Expected electricity ends
Vaccine volumes vanish
Critical components contaminated

Youth's yearnings yielded
Homebound halting harm
Loss, loneliness linger
Battling besieged brightness…

Variants

Mutations of SARS-CoV-2
After their country named;
UK, South Africa, Brazil and India...
Until this nomenclature shamed

Genetics' structures
The formal convention used;
B.1.1.7; 501.V2; P1; B.1.617.2...
Leaving most hopelessly confused

Another convention found
Thanks to the Greek alphabet;
Alpha, Beta, Gamma, Delta...
Different name... same threat

How many more variants
Will challenge the vaccines?
Pfizer, Moderna, Sinovac, J&J...
Will they fight new spike proteins?

No matter what the variants are called
They leave destruction in their wake;
North, South, East, West...
Loss, pain and heartache.

Regrets

If only...

Corruption had not tarnished the City of Gold
Melting it into a statue of dysfunction

Scorched hospitals were repaired in haste
To have beds if the "in case" occurred

Citizens had not dropped their masks
Believing the tide had gone out forever

Many had stayed home that... one... time
When their cabin fever raged within

Vaccine rollout had not been delayed
Saving souls from their untimely passings

Those who were eligible for the miracle jab
Did not forsake it, in the name of hocus-pocus...

We could turn back the sands of time
And wish away our deep regrets

We would learn from the sorrows of the past
And rise from the waters that engulf us.

Minds, Bodies and Souls

Minds doing more:
Thinking... when will this end
Feeling... loss they can't transcend
Wanting... contact with their friend
Remembering... times they did spend.

Bodies trapped in their:
Country... on the "red" list
Province... so spread won't persist
City... with illness in its midst
Home... families striving to coexist.

Souls leaving:
Worlds... in their prime
Loved ones... before their time
Places... for the more sublime
Temples... no more steps to climb.

Luck

Living half a century of luck
Until humanity came unstuck;

Progress in many dimensions
Discarding archaic conventions;

The globe's overall wealth grew
Witness to many a breakthrough;

Child mortality rates fell
Adults were for longer well;

Death seemed reserved for the old
Lifespans increased twofold;

There seemed no end in sight
Until the world took fright…

In eighteen months of awe and shock
Four million souls have left their flock;

Cries of anguish for those departed
Leaving those behind broken hearted;

Worry and sickness, lives pervade
Of the unseen, all are afraid;

Being kept unnaturally apart
Rising poverty has made a new start…

And yet in moments of despair
Of giving up we must beware;

There is so much to be grateful for
While waging this Invisible War;

Vaccines developed at a record speed
Saving millions who'd otherwise be in need;

With masks and distance, keep out of harm's way
Staying healthy — month-by-month, day-by-day;

The selfless and caring saving others' lives
Trying to ensure everyone survives;

Technology enabling communication
Between spouse, partner, friend, colleague and relation...

In a different time, era and space
Our luck would have had a different face;

There is much we must appreciate
Take what we have and protect our fate.

Weeping

Was not a cry with only tears and hurt
But a wailing weep with sadness so sore

A disgraced leader, behind bars
Yet some sent to settle the score

A fire of revenge stoked by sycophants
Scorched the earth after igniting the war

Burnt out trucks, then mobilised mobs
Thieves breaking down door after door

Frenzied looting, cars waiting their turn
Perverse display of esprit de corps

Law enforcement feeble and absent
Only words decrying actions to abhor.

The sobs and heartache are for the loss
Of lives counted by the mortician

Property lost, the poor and now unemployed
Jobs and businesses out of commission

The failures of the state to protect and defend
Lack of intelligence to see this premonition

Interruption of the vaccine program
Increasing rates of COVID-19 transmission

"We told you so," the naysayers loudly declare
Their doomsday predictions coming to fruition

Investment drying up for fear of loss of capital
Scared of being caught in a vortex of demolition.

Yet, when we pause and catch our collective breath
Reflect on the trial and tribulation

Grateful for those who declared "Not in our name"
Who did not succumb to the agitation

The neighbours who stood together to protect
Taxi drivers parked to stop confrontation

Those who reclaimed the ill-gotten property
Volunteers who cleaned up the decimation

Health care workers attending to the injured
The generous who have made a donation

The lament will end and needed change must come
Let's take our resolve and rebuild this nation!

If Only...

Fortunate to have a weapon
To fight this modern-day scourge
Yet you don't believe you need it
Even if conscripted

Your mind made up
Convinced you're invincible
Better to be attacked
Than go on the defensive

Taking sides
Putting myth before science
You're cannon fodder in a battle
That won't win the war

And then you get drafted
Not knowing who called you up
Now you don't have a choice
You'll need to do battle

Injured in combat
Believing your injury
Will heal like others
Who have come before you

When your wounds fester
You expect the medics
To do everything they can
To save you

Yet you wouldn't protect yourself
When you had the chance
You whisper your last words
If only…

Winning

The Pandemic caused a year-long delay
Athletes anxious to have their day
Against all odds, The Games are now in play
In empty stadia, the best talent on display

Spirits lifted by singular success
Records broken in the pursuit of progress
Excellence in action can only but impress
Helping millions forget their current distress

It's not only about winning gold
But the camaraderie we behold
The human body taken to the threshold
Respect for the mind increasing tenfold

When the virus seems to be winning the race
It's reassuring to see humanity set the pace
With guts, gumption, gusto and grace
Olympians show how to claim our place

As many across the globe compete
In a contest to overcome and defeat
We are inspired by the sports' elite
Exemplifying what it takes to beat.

Hesitancy

A euphemism
Called "hesitancy"...
Those rejecting the vaccine
Using unsubstantiated criticism

Governments spending millions...
Lotteries, social media influencers
Adverts, exposés of liars
To convince their civilians

This modern-day miracle
Billions of doses given
So many staying healthy
Data so empirical

Yet, facts don't do the trick...
Fear of deprivation, denial of entry
To a destination of choice
It's not the carrot — but the stick

Refusal is a selfish act
No consideration for others nor self
Not knowing when infected
How the body will react

Not thinking about loves ones
One could leave behind
The gaping holes in the lives
Of daughters and sons

Put aside the misconception
Be part of the solution
No more excuses or denials
Time to stop objection!

Liberty

Clinging to a plane taxiing down the runway
Hanging onto hope as it slips through their hands
Twenty years of freedom banished in a day
Thousands trying to get out to other lands

Scenes of sheer desperation witnessed on TV screens
Walls and barbed wire separate the lucky ones
Leaving needs some luck, the right papers or means
Others now live under the conquest of guns

Fault found and intelligence sources doubted
Who's to blame for the chaos that does ensue?
The soldiers who let their country be routed?
The former saviour with its sudden adieu?

There's a price to pay to protect and defend
One must be answerable to one's own fate
For liberty, on oneself one must depend
Eventually carrying one's own weight

With liberty disappearing so vividly
It sharpens the appreciation one needs
Reminded it can be taken viciously
Should be protected through responsible deeds.

Youth

Like a thief in the dark of night
You've stolen some of their best years
The fearful world took wide-eyed fright
Lockdowns limited their frontiers

Trips disappointingly deferred
Time to see and explore curtailed
Being stuck safe at home preferred
Clipped wings — they feel like they've been jailed

Cancelled concerts, matches and games
No more parties around the clock
Amused on phones and TV frames
Connect via "Insta" and Tik-Tok

It's hard to flirt wearing a mask
No hugging in case you infect
A first date, difficult to ask
When contact barriers in effect

On-line learning the current norm
Replacing class interaction
Rather be wearing uniform
Than have digital distraction

Anxiety always feeling
Anger and rage pent up inside
Hearing of the sick and healing
But also of those who have died

36

COVID in sites close and far-flung
Here to stay if we tell the truth
You must be restrained for the young
To give them back their long-lost youth.

Convince

What will it take to convince?
How much more evidence?
Stories that make one wince
Data points that facts evince

The human condition
Prone to suspicion
Blind to tradition
Lethargic cognition

One's own rights — don't infringe
Yet on others can impinge
Pretence to make others cringe
Of guilt, not even a twinge

For the mind to amend
Need money to spend
Energy to expend
Cajole to no end

We're all in this together
Everyone in no small measure
To beat the viral aggressor
Tame the changes in the weather

Stop listening to every lie
The truth there to clarify
Do your bit to comply
No more need to defy!

Twenty Years on...

9/11 etched in our collective minds...
The Big Apple shaken to its core
Commercial planes turned
Into startling weapons of war

Those dastardly deeds...
The foe had a discernible face
Hunted in foreign lands
Yet, disappeared without a trace.

Ten years later...
Enemy Number One
Caught and killed
No more places to run

With this common cause...
The people were united
Focused on this source of evil
Eradicated and indicted.

Twenty years on...
An adversary in our midst
Invisible and implacable
New variants persist

This nemesis is pervasive...
No agreement on how it to defeat
As we turn on one another
Using spite, ignorance and deceit

To win a battle takes common resolve...
Shared trauma or individual grief
To be channelled to overcome
Provided there is shared belief.

Mandate

Too many to ventilate
Thousands to resuscitate
Millions have met their untimely fate

To vaccinate?
Still so much debate
Individuals' rights to contemplate.

Don't discriminate
Be careful to not dictate
Need to prevent infecting a workmate

Allow staff to procrastinate
Possibly contaminate
Finally, a stalemate...

Mandate
Compulsory to participate
Otherwise employment will terminate

Want to negotiate?
Less room to remonstrate
Employer will try accommodate.

No time to vacillate
False claims must repudiate
No doomsday to prognosticate

For the virus to eradicate
Responsibility cannot abdicate
One more move to checkmate...

Supply Chain

Nando's closed
Bare shelves
Empty fuel tanks
Rationing imposed

Chip shortage
Car sales stall
Prices rising
Postponed portage

Military assisting
Dearth of truckers
Jobs on offer
Workers resisting

Changes to trade
e-Commerce soaring
Suppliers diversified
Containers delayed

Domestic capabilities
Need self-sufficiency
Stockpile critical inputs
Build new facilities

Global supply chain
Weak links exposed
New policies and plans
Will alleviate the strain.

Choices

Routine or unforeseen
Regular or singular

Honest or biased
Illuminated or manipulated

Emotions or notions
Statistics or heuristics

Free or by decree
Egocentric or altruistic

Suspicious or judicious
Rational or unreasonable

Vexing or perplexing
Hobson's or Sophie's

Ingenuous or contemptuous
Painstaking or unthinking

Positive gain or negative pain
Short-term effect or long-term regret…

Voices… expressed by choices
Today's selections creating future directions…

Booster

A booboo
To boo
A booster

Apply for
Approval...
Appraised

Efficacious...
Small effort
Big effect

Immunity
Impeded...
Immunise

Implore
The imperious...
Impose?

Apprehensive?
Appreciate
The apposite

A boon
To book
A booth

Implement
Impactful
Imperative!

Borders

When borders suddenly closed —
A total industry felled;
Travel restrictions imposed
Entry permits were withheld

Vehicle hire, hotels, planes
Precipitous drop in demand;
Affected by various strains
Trips and journeys to countermand.

As border gates were unsealed
A tiny trickle traipsed through;
Some restrictive rules repealed
First indications of déjà vu

Vaccination proof essential
To quarantines must adhere;
Special permit a credential
Non-compliance results severe

"Zero-COVID" course of action
Cancelled by practically all;
Isolation losing traction
Entries through the boundary wall

Border crossings more widespread
The shot offering protection;
More travel to look to ahead
Must not stray from our direction.

Reckoning

Five million souls have left to meet their maker
Leaving loved ones to another caretaker.

Meanwhile on terra firma days of reckoning
Retribution for bad behaviours beckoning

The tip of Africa, politics upended
New parties the local elections contended

Many staying away as a form of protest
A sign to their councillors how much they detest

The once mighty — fallen below fifty percent
Just desserts — their breach of trust and moral descent.

In the West — Senate trial in Pindorama
Criminal charges backed in days of high drama

A report upheld accusing the President
How he the COVID crisis did misrepresent

Ignominy list — crimes against humanity
Nine other wrongdoings — denied by his vanity

The prosecutor-general is his good friend
Will he this "charlatan" indict and apprehend?

Sooner or later others will show their reactions
There comes a time one must account for one's actions.

Cures

When no known solution exists
Humankind looks for another use;
Take what works for other diseases
And these drugs then re-introduce

When the Dragon first spewed its fire
Repurposed hydroxychloroquine;
While it had worked against malaria
Hoped it would counteract COVID-19

Ivermectin a remedy
Successful against parasites;
False claims made in papers and studies
How it the SARS-CoV-2 virus fights

Poor clinical results observed
High concentrations being prescribed;
Toxic effects on people's systems
Many overdoses described

Why desire these bogus cures?
There's a way to offer protection;
Vaccines accepted by billions
To stop the dreaded infection

Do not believe the phoney claims
Deceived that they today's scourge can heal;
Prevention is the route to follow
Even when cures are real.

Junior Jab

Would your kid take a fab jab from a lab?

If you a lad, go ask dad if he's had

If you a miss, it's amiss to dismiss

It's time to let you go get — it's all set

If you a fan — no more ban — now you can

Land after land gives command to expand

From five — age to take the stage to engage

Don't forbid a child from saying "I did"

Stop the spread and dread — you'll be in good stead

Inject, protect — limit the Bug's effect!

Whiplash

After braving three major speed bumps
The tarnished road had been much smoother

Not much traffic to spoil the journey
Short glances in the rear-view mirror

The destination in view ahead
Almost close enough to touch and smell...

Smash! Crash! Whiplash!
Crunch! Scrunch! Gut punch!

Happened so fast
Stopped in my tracks

Craning my neck
Turning to see

At first don't know what caused the damage...
The culprit's identity revealed

Know the pain is going to get worse
Hoping the known remedies will work

As the shock and disbelief wear off
Going to have to sit tight and wait...

Focal Point

The once heady days of Nelson Mandela gone
Citizens battling daily — barely hanging on

Ravaged by wasted years of corruption and cronyism
Plagued by battles of inequity and racism

The new dawn interminably deferred
Lockdowns seeing greater damage incurred

Waiting for the days when S.A. will be in the press
Other than for stories which distress and depress.

But, alas, this was not to be when all eyes turned
Focal point and bad memories of being spurned

Headlines about a new strain all over the news
Who's to blame? It's too easy to surmise and accuse

Local world-class science not fully appreciated
More evidence is needed for a world deflated

Exponential increases daily in new cases
Omicron now appearing in far and wide places

We hunker down again, hoping to evade
Our return to better times, once more delayed...

Be Gentle

Tired eyes and minds
Tested by the abnormal
Taken to the limit
Trying to cope

Stressed by uncertainty
Sick if exposed
Some are silent
Society too scary

Digital overexposure
Demands unrelenting
Day and night blurred
Deliver or dismissed

Prices continually rising
Pressure on the purse
Products in short supply
Patience perpetually tested

Fragile citizens
Fearing breaking point
Fantasising about the future
Facts too hard to fathom

Mired in negative thoughts
Messy mental states
Movement curtailed
Moments feel like months

Be gentle…
Behind every mask
Beats a heart with
Buried thoughts…

Wildfire

The hot wind from the South blew
Whooshing the spark up the flue
Different in form and hue
How far would its flashes spew?

Its existence striking dread
Trying to stop its quick spread
Turning back those who had fled
How plans were turned on their head.

Told to make a firebreak
Some believed this to be fake
Naïve to possible heartache
How much they may well forsake.

Travelling at lightning speed
Scorching earth itself to breed
New grounds found on which to feed
How quick till it will exceed?

Its damage is still in doubt
Unknown is its strength and clout
It'll ultimately burn out
How long till the final rout?

Relief

As the holiday season drew near
It seemed there could be so much to fear
A new variant identified here
Maybe there would not be much Xmas cheer?

While Omicron is so much more contagious
Its lack of virulence is advantageous
Feared hospital admissions so outrageous
Policies decided which were courageous

Early fear and panic nations gripped
Frenzied froth on this novel wave whipped
Urgent calls for ambulances slipped
Count of ventilation cases dipped

Millions chosen on vaccines to depend
Boosters approved which can protect and defend
More tools helping the virus to apprehend
Need to appreciate what's been a godsend

Breathe a collective sigh of relief
As we hold onto the cloverleaf
Hoping its now fourth stay will be brief
It will require more than just belief...

Time

It's infinite — yet defines the finite
Each instant stamped by its ever-ticking clock

While each moment is set to a beat
It can pass in a flash or an age

Events recorded for posterity's sake
Feelings transient in each experience

Powerless to change its constant rhythm
Wasted wishes for it to pass more quickly.

The year twenty twenty-one now done
Etched in the annals of history

Living through its constant chime
Often slowed — wave after wave

Numbers leaving their trail of evidence
Related pain in invisible ink

As living hearts beat to its cadence
May it pass as hopes and dreams come true…

Rights

A year of rights
Do what you deem;
To set your sights
Do as you scheme

So you wrongly thought
As the year rolled in;
You would not get caught
No matter the sin

You stir up turmoil
Rise up and rebel;
Others castigate
Sounding the death knell.

Spread untruths and lies
Despite the science;
Not a care who dies
In your defiance

Evidence reveals
Your masked hidden face;
The layers peeling
Exposing disgrace

Abusing by doing wrong
Privileges and powers;
Your jaundiced views don't belong
In your ivory towers.

You have the right to choose
But when you found wanting;
Put away your excuse
And begin confronting…

Control

Thought we would stem its high tide
Through lockdowns and travel bans
Keep control over its spread
But it had different plans

Its contagion unmatched
Million plus in one day
Takes control of our worlds
Infecting easy prey

As the Big "O" looks to afflict
Scary, deathly stare less severe
Gains control of our warm bodies
Unvaccinated more to fear

Travel arrangements in turmoil
Worker shortages where you look
Lose control over schedules
As many wait until it's shook

Hospitals at breaking point
An increase in admissions
Outside the needed control
Of nurses and physicians

The young more vulnerable
Affecting those under five
Wrests control of studying
Lessons lost — online or live

It's still going to take time
For the normalcy we crave
We long to take back control
As we wait for the next wave?

Rules

On court, you follow the rules in your quest for glory
Yet you tried subversion knowing the mandatory
When trying to enter Down Under territory

Finding willing accomplices to help work around
Applying different criteria for the renowned
Briefly consigning you to an immigrant compound

Despite a judge granting you permission to go free
You misjudged the mood and minister who held the key
On grounds of "health and good order" — now a deportee.

In the House, you make the rules for others to follow
Yet exempt yourself from these bitter pills to swallow
Adding to your litany of lies as you wallow

How many more times do you need to apologise?
Conduct forgiven more than most care to memorise
Your blond shock of hair losing lustre as a disguise

The memories of your parties have started to sour
While your nation remembers lockdown hour after hour
How much longer will you hang onto waning power?

As the people grow tired of those who show no respect
Want to see rules applied equally to full effect
Understand they are there for good measure to protect!

Work

The world of work witnessed silent revolution
As times, modes and places found substitution
Offices closed — workers found a new solution
Work from Anywhere — provide a contribution

To home it started with a mass migration
Then any place with internet connection
Tech tools to keep people in conversation
Many without work in their occupation

After a year, began the "Great Resignation"
As new openings saw an acceleration
Workers looking for greater job satisfaction
Many not returning to their old workstation

Staff shortages in many a corporation
Pressure on workers' historic compensation
Pay increases to stop changes of vocation
Adding to the general rate of inflation

The picture is not the same in every location
Some economies still battling with devastation
Unemployed struggling to change their situation
Skilled workers benefitting from digitisation

As investment increases in automation
Demand for latest skills and qualification
Earning a living undergoing transformation
Will workers cope with trial and tribulation?

Companions

As humans hurriedly hunkered down
Behind doors, fences and gates
Not able to venture into town
To socialise with their mates

Companions of a different kind
Fish, furry or feathery
Helped to occupy their time and mind
Distract them from the TV

These special animals in their midst
To cuddle; gaze at; hear cheep
Took the place of many who were missed
As many alone did weep

When suddenly to hug was taboo —
Because they were virus free
They kept a sense of touch between two
Part of what it means "to be"

Unconditional love, others not;
Yet so much more than just pets
Helping many who others forgot
To feel valued as assets

The risk starts to increase of neglect
As closed worlds reopen once more
These valued friends we need to protect
Their fate we cannot ignore.

Take-out / Take-in

When locked up at home for weeks on end
Trying a virus to apprehend
On what food will you and yours depend?

Your stomach starts to rumble
Your mouth gives off a grumble
Want chow that's more than humble

Home-based cooking can feel like such a chore
It's not always easy to get to a store...
Call an e-delivery service to your door

Grubhub, Uber Eats and Doordash
Delivering fare in a flash
All via apps — no need for hard cash

While helping restaurants from closing shut
Some eateries' earnings punched in the gut
E-companies taking a sizable cut

As the world slowly starts opening up
Many still not keen to eat out close-up
Feel safer not to venture out to sup

New tech has turned dining out on its head
Eating in preferred with its greater spread
Time will tell where we would like to be fed.

Protests

Mandates for truckers required
The golden maple syrup soured;
Protests swelled in the capital
"Freedom Convoy" impassable;
Joined by many disaffected
Saying their rights not respected;

Bi-national trade stopped
Bridge border crossing blocked;
Auto industry impact
City's good image cracked;
Children put in harm's way
Parents' shields — not to play;

Emergency Act invoked
Right to free protest revoked;
Funds raised for protests frozen
New cop chief to be chosen;
The city less congested
As many now arrested.

In the land of the long white cloud
The first city under a shroud;
Protests on lawns of parliament
Non-vaxxers with their argument;
"Macarena" and "Baby Shark"
Failed to disperse those in the park.

Allow citizens freedom of speech
How to determine when overreach?
When rights of others not borne in mind
Hate, violence and mischief assigned;
It's also how leadership engage
For protests to end in peace or rage.

Power

The Invisible War fades into the background
Overtaken by the bellicose bombs unbound

Another example when power goes unchecked
Conflict and conflagration — should come to expect

It starts with bad deeds against those in direct sight
Arrests, exile, poisonings and murder their plight

Over time, minority civil rights suppressed
Opposition parties quashed; foreign lands annexed

Outwitting most others while playing his long game
Expertly camouflaging his ultimate aim

Lies and deception — every trick in the spy book
More flagrant abuses as he gets off the hook

Bolstered by historic military success
He now strikes — aiming to cause maximum distress

He sees a noble future across the frontier
While its citizens live every moment in fear

Their sovereignty threatened while under attack
Showing resistance to the Bear as they fight back

A sad, bewildered world looks on demoralised
With years of evidence, it should not be surprised

Will strong sanctions be enough to force a retreat?
Too much pride to allow any form of defeat

The ending of this chapter should make us all quake
Despots have always left destruction in their wake.

The Chess Game

As the Grand Master
You have more pieces on the board
Outwitting your opponents for over two decades;
As you still have much to prove
You prepare for your next move

You send your Pawns in
Stopped by Knights in shining armour
With their jumping agility they put up resistance;
Your steps surprisingly slowed
You threaten another mode

You make a mistake
Bishop moved out of position
The whole board almost destroyed by a nuclear explosion;
Tritely blame the other side
The millions who could have died

You deploy your Rooks
Move up and down the rank and file
Civilians trying to outrun attacks they know will come;
Can't believe a word you say
Scared to look the other way

Your advantage clear
Greater force at your disposal
Underestimate how the other side could use its Queen;
Moves in any direction
Could change the game's complexion

Your warped worldwide view
Shapes the play of this fatal game
Wanting to create more subjects under your rule as King;
Will you go on to dictate?
Or will someone call checkmate?

Hero

Starting your career being funny
Comedy shows to make your money;
Playing a president who taught youth
Later turning fiction into truth

From afar, your win deemed a bad joke
Yet the voice of democracy spoke;
Your people — weary of corruption
Believed you would bring transformation

Your cunning neighbour now lay in wait
Categorising you as lightweight;
The moment now ripe for his grand scheme
Take over and make you a has-been

But as the clock struck the hour zero
You emerged an unlikely hero;
Asked for ammunition, not a ride
Reflecting your iron-will and pride

Inspired other peoples and your own
Galvanised support — battling alone;
A leader with great courage and grit
Fighting for freedom, refuse to quit

Your honed craft of communication
Rousing words beyond your own nation
Churchillian natured phrases broadcast
Ovation for your words so steadfast

As you come under sustained attack
And the odds of war against you stack
Your foe wants to read your epitaph...
The free world hopes you'll have the last laugh!

Casualties

In the bewilderment of war...
Casualties lie strewn
Across lands now fallow
Bereft of their losses

Truth buried beneath...
Lies of concocted yarns
Woven to entrap
The unknowing minds

Consciences tainted...
Blinkered fence sitters
With vested interests
Taking myopic decisions

Economies battered...
Blows to supplies
Spiralling prices
Bruised consumers

Soldiers sacrificed...
On the altar of folly
Sent into battle
Conjured casus belli

Children's innocence...
Snatched like a toy doll
Discarded in the rubble
Never to be returned

Refugees routed...
Into worlds unknown
Fleeing the future
To what will they return?

Lives of all ages...
Will not reawaken
Shattered pictures
Of what was... and will never be...

What waste we witness...
Victims of a malevolent mind
A reality created
Of unwanted consequences.

The Drumbeat

Again, a war where blood has soaked the earth,
Many fleeing the harsh, angry weapons;
With each new night more hunger, greater dearth,
"Safe" hiding places destroyed in seconds.

Cities pummelled into mortar and bricks,
The brave fighting to defend each square mile;
Monger motivated by politics,
His nefarious aims camouflaged in guile.

The survivor shakes her weary head,
Memories of eighty years ago stirred;
Never believed she again would feel dread,
Forgotten sounds for decades unheard.

No matter the years of relative peace,
War's dastardly drumbeat shall never cease.

Two Years on...

Two years since filling the blank screen
Time to reflect — review the scene:

More than six million bade farewell
The virus being their death knell

Lives ended while still in their prime
Will not know the fullness of time

Too many left alone at night
Still coming to terms with their plight.

Different strategies deployed
Lockdowns and vaccines employed

The red dragon is held captive
By a disease so adaptive

Other nations living more free
Inoculation is their key.

Faces hidden behind a mask
Sowing doubt about who to ask

Heightened anxiety and fear
From sudden traumas so severe

Cautiousness — a way to behave
Mindful of yet another wave.

Massive move to digital tools
Social, fun, work and on-line schools

Some deprived of this way to learn
Lessons missed — cause of great concern

Workers now work from anywhere
More choice for some, others despair.

Humbling much of humanity
The virus bared our vanity

Still those who believe in a war
For their lost glory to restore

A time passed — stranger than fiction
End soon these days of affliction?

The Human Spirit

One hundred surreal weeks
Living through troughs and peaks;
In this passage of time
The absurd; the sublime

A virus, hate or war
To end what was before;
Resilience is within
To once again begin

So many lessons learnt
Moments you wish weren't;
New insights to apply
Through a more expert eye

No matter what the odds
Prayers to beseech the gods;
Better future through hope
Inner strength to help cope

Love has the strong power
To transform sweet from sour;
Feeling that you belong
See right — not only wrong

The want to overcome
Refusing to succumb;
No matter what the strife
It's the will to live life!